CONFESSIONS OF A GEMINI: THE D.A.M.E EDITION© 2018 by Katrice Sterling. All rights reserved.
Published by Vantage Point Publishing
Indianapolis, IN 46226

No part of this publication may be reproduced or transmitted in any form or by any means, electronic or mechanical, including photocopy, or any information storage and retrieval system, without permission from the publisher. The only exception is a brief quotation in printed reviews.

Limit of Liability/Disclaimer of Warranty: While the publisher and author have used their best efforts in preparing this book, they make no representations or warranties with respect to the accuracy or completeness of the contents of this book and specifically disclaim any implied warranties of merchantability or facilities for a particular purpose. No warranty may be created or extended by any persons. The advice or strategies herein may not be suitable for your situation. You should consult with a professional where appropriate. Neither the publisher nor author should be liable for any loss of profit or any other incidental damages, including but not limited to special, consequential, or other damages.

This is a work of fiction. Names, characters, businesses, places, events and incidents are either the products of the author's imagination or used in a fictitious manner. Any resemblance to actual persons, living or dead, or actual events is purely coincidental.

ISBN 978-1-943159-26-0

Dedication

For anyone that is fighting battles, no one knows about it.

This is for you.

Panera (4/29/18)

It's like my sleeping pattern is all outta whack. I can sleep all day and still wake up and be tired. I guess this is what depression looks like. Some days are better than others. I hate that one day I can be okay and the next I doubt my existence just from one thing going wrong. Today I'm not sure how I feel. Currently doing laundry, cleaning up my room and attempting to lift my spirits. Going to meet up with someone later who was once heavily important to me. We speak occasionally. I met her when I was around 14/15. Now I'm 29. Crazy how time flies, right?

Throughout my teenage years and early 20s, she was my mentor/big sis She's married with a kid. A lot has changed over the years and I guess life has somewhat gotten in the way. I moved away for 4 years and I came back to the city last August. Needless to say, I don't really keep in contact with anyone anymore. I literally stay to myself and mind my business. Anyway. I got a text last night when I woke up outta my sleep. "Hey love, I've been thinking about you for the last two days and I pray all is well. When can I see you?" I responded tomorrow.

So, today we're linking up at Panera. I'm not sure how this gonna go. I hope I don't have an emotional breakdown. ☹ Ironically, I'm always everyone's "baby". Lol. So, in her eyes I hope she can see I'm no longer the teenager she met back in 2004.

I'm an adult that is currently struggling and dealing with a lot. I'm hoping she also has some time to spare and doesn't have to rush off. I just need to be loved on, even if it's momentarily. She's one of those people that I'll always admire because whether she knows it or not; she has help mold me into the woman I am today. Even if I feel some type of way or sad because we don't talk as much as we used to...I'll always love her. ALWAYS ➡ ALL WAYS. Most relationships that I have maintained for many years are like that. I used to feel some type of way for the longest about why I don't talk to certain folks for an extended period of time. But, the older I get I understand that, LIFE 💐 HAPPENS!

Sometimes or if not often, we go thru shit. Sometimes we don't have anything to say. Sometimes it just it what it is. Sidenote: I should really pray today. My heart is heavy and I feel unbalanced. Unfortunately, that's almost every day for me...🥴

Lemme go ahead and claim it: One day in the near future I WILL find peace again...

. Turning 30? I know it's a blessing. But, yoooooooo...I do not have my shit together. I'm beginning to wonder if I ever will. Literally the last 6 years, that's all I've been doing. Always working trying to make shit shake. Clearly that's not enough tho...The question is... how do I embrace this chapter I'm about to enter? I can't keep doing the same thing or have the same type of mind set. Is there some type of guideline or rulebook that can outline turning 30? Cuz I'm excited but also nervous...

Things: (5/18/2018)

I am a tomboy. I always have been and always will be. However, I know how to dress when need be. Because I'm always working or going to school...my attire has always been jeans, hoodies, t-shirts, and tennis shoes. That's just where I'm comfortable. I don't have to change who I am or how I dress for anyone. I've always lived by that. Even though I can dress up when need be...I'm still self-conscious. I hate shopping and I only do when I have to. I lowkey get anxiety going shopping. As I've gotten older, it's gotten a little better. I'm normally in and out. I despise going to multiple stores, browsing or even going window shopping. It's hella annoying.

It's crazy that I say that because that's actually what I did today when I got off work. LOL. Last minute preparation for my birthday trip next week. I really need clothes in general, esp for the summer. My wardrobe is limited. 👻 I'm proud of myself tho. I went to at least 4 stores and bought some stuff. Luckily some of the things I got was on sale. The last couple of years I've been attempting to step out of my comfort zone. Like wearing more dresses, bolder colors, and more tightness. ☺ So, this time around was no different. I got some shirts, a dress, a romper and a couple of pairs of shorts. Pretty good, right?

I thought so. 🙃 I realize tho when I try on clothes that I'm def self-conscious. my legs are beat up, I have body acne, I feel fat, cellulite etc. I just feel uncomfortable in general. But, I fight thru the negative feelings and buy what I like. Breaking comfort zones is hard. Anyway. I come home to lay everything on my bed, try my stuff on, and see what's what. I'm pretty happy with all I purchased. I harassed my mom and she just started the nonsense. Asking me how much weight I lost, telling me how I need to wear my clothes and just being overly obnoxious. I guess it hurts my feelings that she never says anything positive. She ALWAYS points out the obvious. Thanks, ma...I know I've picked up weight, I know my face is broken out etc. It might not seem like a big deal to others but to me it hurts. And makes it look like my mom is from hateration nation. Like I said previously, I'm already self-conscious...and my mom saying all this shit doesn't help me. Ultimately it's how about I feel about myself. Just lemme be great, damn!!!!

Despite all that I know what I'm capable of and I feel comfortable with what I bought. It's for me and not her. I'm just proud of myself that I'm breaking my norm. But I'll always feel safe in some jeans, chucks, and a hoodie.

Last 29 (5/22/2018)

Currently out at a bar...had a terrible drink, mini tacos, and cheese cubes. My last 15 minutes as a 29 year old. I feel calm. A sense of peace, also excitement. I'm not sure what the chapter of my 30s will hold...but I'm hoping it will be amazing. When I was younger, I always imagined what my life would be like at 30. And, I'm doing nothing like I imagined. I'm okay with that. I'm understanding that timing is everything. I've taken hella losses in this chapter I'm about to close. But, I've also learned a lot as well. So, cheers to this new chapter. I'm praying I continue to make lemonade with lemons. Embrace everything that's thrown at me....the good, the bad, the ugly. Meanwhile, learn how not to worry and stress less. Continue to work on a better me...so that I can be the best version of myself possible. I like who I am. So, with that being said....cheers to a new chapter!

NOLA (5/27/2018)

It's my last day in New Orleans. Of course I'm up earlier than my friends. I've taken a shower and about to gather my things so that I won't have to try and scurry and get them together later. Our flight doesn't leave until 330pm. We have to be checked out by 12, so we have a little time. As I'm sitting here reflecting....I'm not sure how to feel. I don't think 30 has hit me just yet. I thought that it did, but it hasn't.

This trip has been fun. Interestingly enough, I thought it would be a lot more turnt than what it was. 😄 I mean, my friends and I were pretty much on the same wave. We took the necessary naps, got drunk every day, and most DEFINITELY ate good. I think it's just a vital break for all of us. So now, after 4 days of not having to give a fuck about anything...I'm headed home back to reality. ☹

On my actual birthday, I got some news which started off good and then ended up bad. It rocked my world that day. I've been doing my best not to dwell on it too much, because I know that everything happens for a reason. It just sux because I really wanted the situation to work out. With that being said, I'm hesitant to go back home cuz I don't want bad things to keep happening. Sounds crazy, right? Well, in my head it makes sense. LOL.

Realistically, I gotta go harder than ever before. Because now? Time is of the essence. And, I have to know that one bad result on my birthday shouldn't represent the rest of my 30s being terrible.

STILL: (8/27/2018)

It's never ending. My thoughts often control me. What did I do right? What did I do wrong? Can I fix it? The answer is NO. My past haunts me & I don't know how to move on from it. I broke someone's heart not once, but TWICE. I think about him every day. Certain songs remind me of him. Specific spots make me feel some type of way. It's hard for me to go to Chicago now, because I know he lives there. I feel like I fucked up so terribly that I'll never find someone like that to be in a relationship with again. I KNOW that's not true. ☹ BUT, I guess I mean it in the sense that....no one will be able to relate to me like him. No one will do the things he did for me, like him. Once again, I know it's NOT true. But, subconsciously that's how I feel. A part of me feels like I'm not worthy. This is when dysfunction & baggage comes into play. Every time I think of what I want in a man, he's it. Granted he has flaws just like every other person in this world...but still. I think my mindset is this way because he was my first real relationship in my adult life. It's sad that I'm 30 & I've only legit had one serious relationship. ☹ *Kanye shrug*.
I know I should eventually get back out there but nahhhh. I know the reasons I had to end it; but, a part of me is coming up with excuses as if it was valid or not. I partially

regret it & that's only because I miss him so much. We are not meant to be together. That I know but it still doesn't help me from being heartbroken & him hating my guts. I'm not blameless in this matter, because I definitely have my shit. I have a smart mouth, I can shut people out without any notice, and be brash. At one point and time he told me that I was mean, rude, and disrespectful. I have my moments but I'm not a bad person by any means. With that being said, I have a lot of unlearning to do. When you know better, you do better. I keep so much to myself. I've never experienced love in the rarest form. All I've ever had is myself. So, when all you've ever had is YOU...how do you process loving someone and them loving you back? It's a hard pill to swallow knowing we're not meant to be together & that I ended it. He was my best friend. My confidant. My homieluvahfriend. My support. My encouragement.

I know I need to let this go but I can't. Hell, I even wanna send him some beard butter for his birthday in a couple of weeks. Don't judge me. 🙊

I really need to work thru this & let him go. I just don't know where to begin & a piece of me doesn't want to. In the meantime I'll pray for healing, clarity, and peace. I know whoever is meant for me will be for me. Or at least that's what I gotta keep believing while I work thru my shit...Please pray my strength. I wanna learn how to love someone properly and accept someone loving me in my entirety. But, in order to do that I gotta love me first...

Decompress: (8/30/2018)

Like usual, I'm doing too much. My mind won't turn off or turn down. The wheels keep spinning like some 24's. A lotta good things happening. A lotta uncertainty. A lotta faith. A lotta strength. A lotta patience. A lotta exhaustion. I wish those that knew me could live inside my mind for a day. There's no way to exactly explain anxiety or how it makes someone feel. Imagine ALWAYS being worried, constantly overthinking, feeling nervous and being obsessed with choices you make. This is everyday life for me. I can't turn this shit off.

I've just learned how to function while dealing with it. How do you become free? I think I've been this way my whole life. I've always been a worry wart. It's just come full-fledged in my adulthood, and I never had a name for it. Working nonstop, planning to move, planning trips, taking life day by day etc. Wanting/needing drastic changes in different areas of my life.... but don't know where to begin. All of it is overwhelming. The only thing that remotely gives me peace is praying. At this point and time, I really wanna decompress, hit a beezy one time, and lowkey be a hippie that doesn't give a fuck. but until then, I'll just vent and hope one day I'll be able to NOT overthink EVERYTHING.

Superheroes: (11/16/2018)

Some people we find to be invincible or we THINK they're invincible. Because they're so strong, fearless, courageous, and just a bomb ass individual. But in reality, we ALL go thru trials and tribulations. There are certain people in my life that are my go to when I am weak and feel less than my best. They help to support me, encourage me, and love on me when necessary. But, who does that for them?

If I haven't talked to one of my "superheroes" in a while; I assume they're doing ok. And that's when the misconception comes in. Whether it is a couple of weeks or a couple of months...

What comes out of my mouth is: "What?? Wait!!! Hol up, when did this happen?!? Are you ok?! Why didn't you tell me??" I automatically feel bad and in that moment, I realize that my superheroes are human too.

Sometimes, if not often their cape needs to be ironed out, tied again, and ready to fly. We all are our own superheroes. And with that being said, let's take care of ourselves. No one is exempt from the bullshit that life throws at us. However, let's be empathetic to not just our superheroes... but everyone. let's choose love in every aspect of the word....

Aim to Please: (11/26/2018)

The new year is upon us. I haven't really thought about it that much. But, now that December is rapidly approaching, I can't help to think about it. I have been 30 for 6 months. I am still embracing and leaving all the mistakes I made in my 20s in the past. I am now focusing on this new chapter. Who am I becoming? What do I want for myself? How do I accomplish goals that seem so daunting? I'm tryna sort thru all these emotions and questions that plague my mind daily. I'm still searching for my happy. What does happiness look like for me?

Tonight, my therapist asked me what my 5-year plan was. I started to give her a cliché answer. I began to tell her the typical answers... like potentially having a baby, getting married, being happy. Then I paused...

I thought about it briefly and was like I really don't know. I told her that every time I plan something...it NEVER works out. It's almost as if I'm attempting to play a trick on God. I also told her that I've learned that planning doesn't necessarily turn out how you want it to. And, I've had to learn the hard way. An easier method for me is to take things day by day. That seems to work better for me. I was once told that the future as we know, doesn't really exist and all we have is the now. I agree with that to a certain extent. It lowkey takes the pressure off of me to have everything figured out. I think at the tender age of 30, I'm understanding and figuring out what it is that I TRULY want for myself. Because all selfish as this sounds...it is all about SELF. I have no kids. No spouse/significant other. Just me. I'm okay with that.

My future seems a little bit brighter when I take those expectations off myself and open up to possibilities/opportunities that I didn't think were obtainable before. My future looks different than what I thought it should be....just from a couple of years ago. I am OK with the now.

I am learning to be unapologetically myself. which for some, is a lifelong journey. it feels like 30 is just the beginning. I am in the beginning stages of becoming the greater version of myself. scary? yes. necessary? hell yes. but...when we know better, we do better...

Freedom: (12/24/2018)

A lot of things have changed in the course of my 20s. Now that I'm 30...it's as if the light has been turned on. I'm finally coming into myself. I'm learning who I am, what I want/need, and just being comfortable with myself. The biggest lesson that will forever be a lifelong journey is UNLEARNING bad habits. I'm done talking about shit, I just do it. For a couple of years now I have been talking about cutting my locs. I said when I turned 30. Part of me has been afraid to do such a major change. But this year, I understood how necessary it was to go thru with it. I started my locs in 2009, when I came home from the Navy. I had them for officially 9 years. My mentor aka my other mom is the one that always did my hair. I've been begging & pleading for her to cut them. She kept telling me no. In November I FINALLY wore her down and she said fine. I was shocked that she actually agreed. Long story, short....up until the day of, I wasn't sure how to feel. I feared what people might say, their reactions & I didn't want to explain my decision. On Saturday, 12/22/2018...it was about to go down! I had made my mind up that I was happy, excited, nervous and ready. On my way to my loctician's house....I had a conversation with God & myself. I was good. I got to her house, and she cut my locs super-fast. The first section she cut, I was like omg!!! She said, "nope you can't turn back now." 😐 She was done in about 15 mins. It was such a crazy feeling to actually rub my hands thru my scalp and SEE my hair this short. Shortly after she washed it and headed to the barbershop. We got there somewhat early too & it was packed. 😐 I waited about 2 hours & then her brother cut it. I can't lie, my anxiety was super high. I kept feeling myself tense up...but at the same time I was doing my damnest to stay calm. He finished in about 40 mins. Went back to her house, and she dyed it. It was really sinking in what I had just did. Overall, I'm glad that I did it. I feel so free. I pray this feeling will roll over into other aspects of my life in 2019. Some might say that this was a drastic decision....but it wasn't. It was planned.

With me cutting my locs after 9 years...it's like I let go of so much dead weight, literally & figuratively. I don't expect other folks to understand. I don't care what people say. At the end of the day, I did it for me & only me. IT ✊IS ✊JUST✊ HAIR!!! It will grow back. I am becoming more comfortable within who I am. I'm cool with it. You ain't gotta agree but you will respect it. It's all about freedom & healing. I'm claiming it in all aspects of my life. And I believe this is the first step in the right direction.

I'm with the shitz. ❤

Processing: (1/20/2019)

Within the last day or so I've been doing some heavy thinking...and my brain just won't turn off. I'm beginning to feel how I felt in 2016/2017. I remember seeing a therapist on campus. I also remember it being therapeutic, scary, and becoming triggered... by opening up about myself and some of the experiences I have been thru. Fast forward...I'm feeling the same. The thing about me is...I function highly with depression and anxiety. Anxiety is a daily bih. And depression? It's always there but some days...it just decides to rear its ugly head. I don't know how or when it comes, it just does. I've been in therapy 2 months and I'm starting to feel the effects of being so transparent. From dealing with issues about my family, a falling out with a friend, and just overall adulting. It all feels so heavy. I'm not saying that I expected therapy to be a one and done situation. But, clearly this healing process is gonna be a lot harder than what I initially thought. I'm also realizing its gonna take time. So many emotions I feel. Mainly overwhelming. I guess I'll pray that God gives me the strength to handle all of this. I know I need it. So much baggage to unpack. I thought I was ready but....I'm not. Better now, than later...I suppose.

This whole process is just hard. Accepting that I know I can be a better a version of myself is...the truth. But getting to this point? It takes courage...and I'm working on it.

Easily: (3/15/2019)

Within the last day or so I've been doing some heavy thinking...and my brain just won't turn off. I'm beginning to feel how I felt in 2016/2017. I remember seeing a therapist on campus. I also remember it being therapeutic, scary, and becoming triggered... by opening up about myself and some of the experiences I have been thru. Fast forward...I'm feeling the same. The thing about me is...I function highly with depression and anxiety. Anxiety is a daily bih. And depression? It's always there but some days...it just decides to rear its ugly head. I don't know how or when it comes, it just does. I've been in therapy 2 months and I'm starting to feel the effects of being so transparent. From dealing with issues about my family, a falling out with a friend, and just overall adulting. It all feels so heavy. I'm not saying that I expected therapy to be a one and done situation. But, clearly this healing process is gonna be a lot harder than what I initially thought. I'm also realizing its gonna take time. So many emotions I feel. Mainly overwhelming. I guess I'll pray that God gives me the strength to handle all of this. I know I need it. So much baggage to unpack. I thought I was ready but....I'm not. Better now, than later...I suppose.

This whole process is just hard. Accepting that I know I can be a better a version of myself is...the truth. But getting to this point? It takes courage...and I'm working on it.

It Never Ends: (3/26/2019)

Some days are better than others. And some days are just blah. A lotta things have changed the last couple of months, and some things have stayed the same. Although I'm feeling lighter these days...some things stay the same. Like a continuous cycle of whatever that may be. For me, it is finances, self-doubt, and my health. You know my therapist often talks about creating new neuropaths for ourselves and leaving the old one behind. It's ridiculously hard. When all you've known the better part of your life is...dysfunction and being in purely survival mode.

I am beginning to understand that it is all in your mind. How do I train my mind to think/speak/believe good things? Deep down I want success, love, happiness, peace, and freedom. But, how can I obtain these things if all my brain knows is negativity? This is a hard transition. For example, all the time I think of how I need to start living a healthier lifestyle and going to the gym. Of course the benefits would be great. However, all I can think of is the all the food I'll be missing out on. It's the same with studying for my A&P (license to work on aircrafts). I've already failed miserably TWICE. I have no motivation to study or even entertain the idea of accomplishing this goal.

Because somewhere deep inside of me I am self-sabotaging...and it's something I can't shake. Knowing good and well....I've invested so much time, energy and MONEY into a life decision. Yet, here I am...90% done with this goal but I don't have it in me to actually finish. I still can't figure out if this something that I REALLY don't want to do or if I'm just really afraid that I CAN actually succeed. Self-sabotage at its finest. To be honest, I think I am afraid because I've been struggling since I turned 19. With no one to push me...all I've ever had is myself. Sometimes that's not enough. There are so many thoughts of doubt in my head but I somehow have to overcome it. My therapist basically told me I owe it to myself to finish this task. I've given her all the reasons why I don't want to finish this goal. And, she's still not tryna hear it. ☹ lol. So she wants me to create a new neuropath for myself. It is beyond difficult speaking and believing positivity into your life, when all you know is the bad. Could I possibly be this dense to somehow think that deep down, I don't deserve the good in life? The answer is yes. I just begin with self and truly understand that I DO deserve all the great and amazing things life has go offer. So, I guess the first step is believing it. Next would be beating up my old toxic neuropath way of thinking. And after that going after my goals, knowing that I am capable of doing/accomplishing anything that I set out to do.

Sitting here typing this is a lot...but I think I needed to see this in real time so I can process.

I'm learning to celebrate all that we are and any small victory that comes our way. So the fact that I actually pulled out my study guide today and my old test papers speak volumes. Pray for me, while I continue to beat down my own dysfunctional patterns/behaviors and create new neuropaths for myself and allows me to see I am CAPABLE.

Why: (3/30/2019)

Do you ever wonder why someone likes you or rocks with you the way that they do? Why they hang out with you? Why they wanna talk to you? What is it about you that's just so special? If you say you don't, you're lying. Lol. I often wonder, esp as of lately. Some people think I'm just this nice, goal oriented, quiet young woman. Others could think I'm mean and unapproachable. Most would say that I'm cool, laidback, and reserved. Which of these are true depends on the day. ..All I want to do is stay mysterious, drink water, mind my business, and live my life. Why mysterious? Because I think it's cool when people don't know a lot about you. You leave much up to the imagination of folks. I like that idea a lot. Think whatever you wanna think about me. But wait, in the back in my mind...what DO you think about me? Should I care? Why do I even want to know what someone else thinks about me?

I'm entering a new chapter soon....31. And, I'm learning more and more NOT to care what people think. I can say that I haven't cared what anyone else says about me. But to be honest, that's a lie. We all care to a certain degree.

With age, maturity and wisdom...comes freedom. Freedom to be our authentic selves. For some it comes easier than others; and for those others...well who's to say... 🙄
The more we experience life with trials/tribulations...we grow, we evolve, and LIVE. Living unapologetically means you are YOU at all times. You don't care who has something to say, esp if it's negative. You shine your light regardless. You find your truth and revel in it. I'm still learning but I like who I'm becoming....

Different Eyes: (7/16/2019)

Happiness. We all strive for peace, love, and happiness. To be real, I don't think I've ever been happy. I've had 'happy' moments and experiences. I may have even at one point been a happy child. But going thru my teenage years up until now... I haven't been happy. Life often times plague me. I self-sabotage. I overthink. I over analyze. I panic. It is never my intention to do these things. But, it is what it is. The last 6 months I have grown drastically. A lot of forgiveness, healing, and evolving has happened. That in itself is a blessing. In this moment, I feel how I did in 2011. I am frustrated. I am tired of being in survival mode. I am anxious. I am overwhelmed. I woke up this morning from a not so great sleep. As I was getting up and began to get ready for work. I looked in the mirror and I saw nothing but sadness on my face and in my eyes. I began to break down in massive tears. I triggered my own self. Still getting ready and looked in the mirror again, and busted out the ugly cry... yet again. I headed to work feeling some type of way. Everyone keeps asking if I'm ok... and I just give em the slow head nod or say, "I'm just tired."

I text my sis something that I should never ever say. She called me 3 mins after that. I quickly walked to the bathroom & as she's talking, I break down in the ugly cry yet again. Can't say I necessarily felt better after the brief convo. I just wanted to stay in the bathroom and keep crying. My eyes have been heavy all day.

I vowed to never get this low or get to this point in life again. Yet, here I am. I have no obligations, except for myself. I sometimes wonder why people are friends with me, why they like me, or what it is that I bring to their life. Would it even matter if I left this world? In reality, I am terrified to die. But, idk what else to do with myself.

I've always said that I know that God has a purpose for me that's bigger and better than anything I've ever seen. However, idk what my purpose is. Idk how to go about finding it. Maybe God is allowing me to hit rock bottom first. It hurts me to even type these words out. I'm just... tired. Ironically, and esp as of lately people have told me that my eyes look different. I guess it's because I can no longer put on the facade that I am ok. I'm not. I haven't had this feeling in 8 years. I never wanted to come back to this mind state. I've been fighting this mental state for almost the past month. But, this morning it hit me like a ton of bricks. I am officially numb.

On my way to work this morning I slightly thought about running my car into the guard rail. I just wanna go to sleep and don't wake up. I'm not sure if I actually mean these words at the moment... but just know I'm in a fog that I can't get out of. I did manage to say a prayer this morning before I walked into work but I still feel the same.

Is the universe tryna tell me something? Does the devil have me under attack? Is this God's way of pulling me closer to him? Cuz at this point... I don't really believe my life will get better. It feels like a never ending cycle of the same shit. I just... don't know anymore.

Scaredy Cat: (8/17/2019)

And another one...*DJ Khaled voice*

That's what I think when I wake up in the morning. Doing my best to continue taking it day by day. My anxiety is still on 100, pretty much all the time but I'm pushing thru. I had the realest epiphany yesterday. I am... scared. I often talk about the person I want to become, but, in actuality I'm afraid. I'm afraid of undoing/unbecoming of everything I am to become who I'm destined to be. Maybe all these trials & tribulations this year is literally to help me undo my current self & becomebetter. To get rid of my negative neuropaths & to build new ones. Possibly to take better care of myself...etc. The thought in itself is beyond terrifying & overwhelming. Like the idea of wanting to be better & do better is GREAT. But, realistically it's not that easy. I guess the key is consistency & discipline, which is where I lack in a major way. But, I just have to keep reminding myself day by day. Literally day by day... because if I think too ahead into the future I begin to spiral. I'm slowly recognizing this about myself. Also, I'm realizing that I need to create boundaries. We're 8 months into the year & I can honestly say so far... 2019 has been a doozy. I can't lie tho... part me still wants to disassociate myself from the world & go MIA. The other part of me is beginning to understand that timing is EVERYTHING. And maybe everything that I've been going thru the last 10 years for this particular moment. I'll always be a scaredy cat in a sense, but I have a little bit of peace knowing that trouble don't last always. Not only that, but if I've been down... the only way to go is up. LOVE.

Revelation 24:7 (9/10/2019)

I remember the days when I hoped/prayed for what I have now. All I've ever really wanted is stability and a peace of mind. To have that is a blessing in itself. There's so much chaos going in the world; that I just wanna take a moment to reflect. I don't have a lot, but I'm appreciate for what I do have. Cuz I remember the days that I didn't and I yearned for it. And I know that I can only go up from here. I'm simple and I don't require a lot to be happy. Although, I understand that happiness comes from within. I'm diligently working on it. And I think the first step is acknowledging what I'm grateful for. Everyday isn't peaches & cream... but I look at the bigger picture and that keeps me optimistic, as well as encouraged. To look around and know that I have a roof over my head, clothes on my back, a decent car, endless opportunities and seemingly healthy. Blessed.

Entertain the Gray: (11/19/2019)

Life as I've known has changed drastically. Someone should cue Young Jeezy x Vacation. The holidays are coming up and I feel meh. On top of that, my peace has been violated and sorely interrupted. I am greatly and utterly drained, emotionally and mentally. I'm doing my best to keep my head above water, but, it's beyond difficult. I have a roommate that's getting on my everlasting nerve, a new job that I'm doing my best to adapt to and of course daily adulting. It feels like it's all a bit.... overwhelming. But, like my therapist said... learn how to entertain the gray. I'm really doing my best to keep that same energy. I can thoroughly appreciate the prayers that folks cover me with. As much as I want to go MIA... I can't. I have to allow myself to be vulnerable and feel what I need to feel. Entertain the gray. The only thing that's keeping me sane at the moment is... God, work, and hanging with my homies. Thank God for the simple things. I just pray for some normalcy sometime in the near future. Like really in the NEAR future. This year has been full of ups/down, and I at least wanted to end it on a good note. In hindsight, there are 40 more days until 2020 so things could relatively change. In the meantime... the only thing I can control is myself and how I react. I'm also continuing to work on things and be the best version of myself possible. Even tho in the process. I'm being lied to, manipulated, and betrayed. With the good, the bad, and the in between.... we still gotta learn how to entertain the gray. Just pray my strength and courage while I work it out for my good....

Windy: (11/27/2019)

Sitting here listening to SiR as the wind thrashes against my window. And as the sun is playing peekabo, I'm lost in my thoughts. I've been waiting a couple of days to process what has been going on in my life. And I still haven't quite wrapped my head around it. I'm not sure if I ever will. Questions have me coming to me nonstop the last 3 days. Just when I thought my life was coming together, everything comes tumbling down in a matter of 5 mins. I'm lowkey annoyed with God to the point that I can't pray. Why would HE give me the greatest opportunity that I've been waiting years for AND then take it away in an instant? WHY?!?! It doesn't make sense, nor is it fair. I've been impatiently patient for my life to turn around. Well, at least to be in a good space and at least feel like I'm going in the right direction. This year has been beyond an emotional mental rollercoaster. Switching jobs, losing friends, gaining friends, working, healing, forgiving, contemplating suicide, sadness, depression, anxiety, frustration, being supportive, landing the greatest opportunity and then losing it within a 2 month time span. 2019 feels like a major blur. However, through it all... I am still standing. The greatest lesson I have learned this year is to literally take it day by day. That last sentence is the only thing that is getting me through at the moment. DAY BY DAY. I'm back to square one and idk where to go from here. Currently working on doing some soul searching to figure out what I want to do with my life. I know that I am officially over working meaningless jobs in general. One thing I have learned the last couple of days is that companies really don't give a fuck about you. AT ALL. Clearly I have to do something in the meantime to pay these bills. But the bigger question remains: What do I want to do that can make me money, keep me stable and allow me to be happy? *Kanye shrug* If I could just be a financially stable nomad that just travels and go to concerts, that would be living the dream but, unfortunately that's not my reality. Even though I can't pray at the moment, I just really wonder what God's plan is for me. Because every time something is going good and I'm able to take 5 steps forward, I get knocked back 20. As much as I want to sulk in the hurt and emotional/mental exhaustion... I can't. As much as I want to go back down this black hole of depression, I can't. I honestly thought this situation was going to emotionally and mentally rock me to the point that I wouldn't be able to bounce back. Clearly that's not true. I'm not gonna say that I'm in the best space at the moment, because I'm definitely not. At this point I just want stability. That's all I've been looking for the last

10 years of my life. I'm not opposed to working hard and grindin' it out. But, when does it end? I'll be 32 in about 6 months and I am terrified. Even though I am terrified, I guess now is the time for me to figure out what it is that I want to do with my life. As cliche as it may sound, I'm beginning to see that its true. Maybe this is why God put me in the situation that HE did. I am beyond exhausted in every since of the word; but taking things day by day is my solution at the moment. I am still disappointed in myself and the situation at hand, but what what else can I do or say? It is officially the past as of 11/23. As much as I wanted this opportunity and for SWA to be the place for me; it wasn't. Man it sucks just thinking about it. I don't wanna tell my friends that shit didn't pan out because that's when the questions come and then you have to relive it all over again. Not only that, but you also have folks rooting for you and excited for you. But, the real ones understand. They understand that things happen and as much as want things to go our way or work out; it doesn't always work out.

Let's just say God has a funny sense of humor. I have yet to find it but hey. LOL. One thing I can say about myself is I'ma always figure out how to 'go get it' regardless of the situation. On the flip side, I am VERY tired of having to go get it and figure it out. But, it is what it is. I'm still on the search of stability... I hope it comes sooner than later. When I think of things in a wider sense; I'm glad I worked on myself this year mentally and emotionally. I can actually allow myself to feel. Even though I feel like this is the end of the road for me, I know it's not. I actually see things for what they are and I'm not too pressed about the future. You know why? Because I have to continue taking things day by day. Please don't get it twisted because every day isn't peaches and cream. It's still a struggle in every sense of the word but I suppose I am maintaining at the moment. Time waits for no one. It keeps going whether we want it to or not. If and when you read this, all I ask is that you pray for me.

Janet Jackson: (1/24/2020)

Controoooollll *Janet Jackson voice*

I don't know why by the word 'control' has been stuck in my mind like the last two weeks. Why? (Insert Kanye shrug). Maybe it's because I am taking control over my life, or at least certain aspects. I'm becoming to realize that once you turn 30+... your fux really do go out the window. You become more self-aware, you know when you're bouta participate in some fuck shit and you can actively call yourself out on it, annnnnddddd you become more settled within yourself but with the intent of consistently improving yourself. Not only that, your circle will begin to shrivel. That's not necessarily the case for me because my circle has been small. Throughout my adulthood my Pops has always told me, "Who is gon be with you, is gon be with you." Makes sense to me and it is also incredibly accurate. My mind is forever going a mile a minute and is a playground for overthinking. I can't help it...it's just the way I'm wired. However, over the last year I've gotten a lot better. Whenever I want to freak out, panic, or overthink....one of my bestest friends tells me: "We just gon go with it." I look at her and say BUT. She stares me down and says it again: "WE JUST GON GO WITH IT." So, I've adopted the policy and I'm just going with it. And with that being said...We all have some type of dysfunctional ways and/or patterns. One of mine is self-sabotage. I know I am not the only one who deals with it. I am doing my damnest to control it. I say this all the time but it's so fucking true: when you are constantly rejected and things don't work it; we often become a pessimist. I'm still working through it. It is definitely a terrifying feeling. Because when something good comes into your life; whether it be an opportunity, a relationship, a job, a friendship...we become hella skeptical. Or at least that's my situation (*cue eye roll*). It is beyond hard not to self-sabotage. To be honest, I am very good at it... matter of fact it should be on my resume. LISSSEENNN LINDA... the struggle is real!!! Lol. I am clear of my intentions tho and I know when I'm about to do or say some fucked up shit. CONTROOOOLLLLLL. Whew chile, Janet be knowin'. I'm not sure of how to break through this negative trait about myself. Maybe I should Google it...I'm sure an extreme about of articles will pop up. On this Friday afternoon/early evening I am wholeheartedly admitting this to myself. The key is I am aware. I want to change it. I want to embrace all the good in my life... even if it's momentary. I don't like being a pessimist, nor self-sabotaging. Never my intention... but we're all human. And with that, I vow to do better and be better ANNNNNDDDD I'ma just go with it. I'ma also be like Nike and JUST DO IT, while taking Auntie Janet's advice to CONTRROOOOLLLLL this shit. Happiness is hard, sometimes we gotta work for it.

6262820: (2/9/2020)

If love is a choice, why am I so nervous and over analytical about it? My stomach feels queasy, mind is racing, and heart beat is increasing rapidly. Baby Jesus, why?!? To be a late bloomer in life makes me itch. Itch, why? Because it feels like I should've had certain experiences more than once by now. Like being in love. I know we can't necessarily predict the future, because it doesn't exist. The most we should do is take life day by day while being present in the PRESENT. With that being said, I know I can't be afraid of the days ahead... all I can do is embrace it & move accordingly. The fear of heartbreak & rejection plagues me. Why is it so easy to tell my good friends I love them; & when it comes to a significant other I OVERTHINK every emotion I have??? Also, add in that I'm a Gemini and hate being vulnerable. It's too early to say sum'n. So I'll just keep my thoughts & feelz to myself. As I'm writing this Sade - Stronger Than Pride is playing. THIS WAS NOT INTENTIONAL. Fawk my life. 🙇‍♀️ We can be our own worst enemies sometimes. But, I'm doing my best to go with it and if it's meant to be, I'll continue to go with it and enjoy the journey ahead.

CJ: (2/22/20)

I'm at work and my job for the night is beyond repetitive; and with that being said I'm lost in my thoughts. I was thinking about my relationship with both of my parents and how they have shaped me, whether good or bad. My thoughts primarily were geared towards my mother. She's been through a lot and seen a lot. I love her to death, she drives me crazy, and I'm somehow just like her but totally different. I have a 50/50 mixture of both of my parents' personality. Thinking of how she raised me, how big my heart is, and the resilience she has... I get from her. I understand that parent's often do the best they can with what they're given. I'm pretty sure she sheltered me because my sister was a wild child. lol. At 31, I can say I was definitely sheltered and didn't find out a lot about life until adulthood., which caused me to find out things the hard way and be a later bloomer. This morning I'm thinking about how she wasn't that present or emotionally/mentally available for me the last 10 years. I remember going months without talking to her... I didn't wanna be bothered. Because sometimes if not often, I equate her to dysfunction and my spirit wants no parts because it is draining, as well as emotionally taxing. I still kinda feel the same but I'm old enough to understand it better. I remember one year... I was so hurt by the holidays. I talked to one of 'mentors' and telling her I wish that my mom was around more. And she simply replied, "Do you think that her presence would really be beneficial to you at this point?" In that moment it hit me... that it wouldn't. It just made me incredibly sad that was my reality. Luckily around this time, my dad had start stepping up to the plate in all aspects. Financially, mentally, and emotionally. I'm so thankful that he did. Because looking back, I needed him more than I could have ever imagined. For her, I'll always be 'big girl' lol. And even now I still have to respectfully check and remind her that I'm a BIG 31 years of age outchea in these streets. Although I wish I could confide in her more without thinking the worst of what she'll say and the potential judgement that will go along with it. I really wish I had a healthier relationship with her and with my sister too. But, it won't happen. Not because I'm being mean or anything but it's my reality and I accept it. I've found out a lot on my own. Some I've learned the hard way.

I am def the opposite of my family. Like polar opposite. I subscribe to peace, love, and healing... not constant drama, misery, and dysfunction. I'll always feel some type of way about it. In the meantime I'm doing my best to break generational curses. The goal is to be better and do better in all capacities in my life. I recently made a major executive decision. I'm keeping it to myself and a select few. It is what it is. I wish I could disclose it to my family without thinking they would potentially have an ulterior motive. *Kanye shrug*

However, I should thank God more often than I do. Because I really have a big heart and I'll do almost anything for people I care about. I only do for those that will reciprocate the same energy. I wish I could do the same for my family... mainly my mom and sister but it won't happen cuz they'll take advantage, whether they mean to or not. Fucked up, right? I know. Stability is all I've ever wanted since I can remember. Even tho it's sad I feel like this... all I can worry about it is me. And pray they get it together before it's too late. I know I'm a great person. I have my mom's great qualities, as well as the bad ones. I am her daughter. Lol. Someone told me once to not judge her, but just let her be. With that being said... I'm still working and healing on myself. I guess a part of me is doing it for her too. Nonetheless, that's my heart and my headache, but I'm just tryna be better. That's what she wants for me anyway. I love her for that.

Facts, B: (2/24/20)

Another nite, I'm lost in my thoughts at work:

Trust. It can take forever to earn and a moment to lose. I've never necessarily had an issue trusting people. I guess I trust people by their actions. I trust myself the most tho. 👤 I'm a pretty solid person. I'm a woman of action. I'm a woman of my word. If I say I'ma do sum'n...I do it. It might take me a while but I'll get it done. I pride myself on that, because most people aren't built that way and it lowkey irks my soul. Lol. But, I have to understand that not everyone has the same thought process as me, as well as a big heart. All of my life I've been trustworthy. People be telling me their business for no damn reason, they trust me with their money, and all of the above. I've always been kinda shocked by this. Idk why. Part of me believes it's because I whole heartedly believe in karma. Also, I suppose I have a comfortable, open and nonjudgmental energy/spirit. So I would never do anything intentional to hurt someone, ESPECIALLY if they trust me.

Last year I had a situation that rocked me, and I guess I'm still dealing with it emotionally. Clearly it wasn't a big deal to this person because they broke my trust and thought everything was cool after one conversation. Sheeeiiittttt, I think not. It takes me longer to process some stuff. One morning I woke up to roll over and literally thought..."damn she really betrayed me, broke my trust, and violated my space" in a day. Like forreal. Nah, FORREAL. You're grown as hell, and we've been rocking since I was a teenager and you do some fucked up shit like this??? It makes me doubt everything our friendship/sisterhood stood for. Clearly she didn't/doesn't respect me or my space. With that being said, I see her for who she really is and it's sad.

Even though we change and evolve everyday... I know who I am. I'm as solid as they get. If I fuck with you... it's gonna be til the wheels fall off. I definitely had to distance myself from her. I still have love for her, but damn Gina! Trust is broken and I'm pretty certain she'll never get it back. I'm a Gemini so I don't play those types of reindeer games. It's a big deal that I don't take lightly. I trust you to be exactly who you are... which is someone I don't fuck with anymore. To be honest, I've never thought about the trust factor in my life because it's NEVER been an issue. I've never had reason to doubt someone. In hindsight, that's definitely a blessing. Some say I should forgive her and move on. Others say fuck her. Even after what she did, I still wish her all the love in the world. But our relationship is indefinitely on the outs, b. Deadass. Meanwhile, I'll continue to keep being me... despite my ill feelings towards her. I forgive you but I'll never eva eva eva EVA forget. I trust myself to keep being a bomb ass individual, loving, genuine, honest, articulate, cute, sassy, and hard working woman. BOOM. Like the homie Jill Scott said, "You hurt me, but I'm healing..." *drops mic*

Tommy Pickles: (2/26/2020)

My anxiety is on 1,000,000 and it has been since last nite. I'm getting some signs from the universe and I honestly dunno how to feel about it. I'm in a pretty good space. Feel'n more & more grown these days. And with that comes making GROWN decisions and putt'n my big girl drawz on. Lol. Everyone knows I overthink & constantly over analyze. It's hindered me in a sense, because, I can never just outright make an executive decision. I have to talk to someone, write it out, and play the scenarios in my head over and over again. I know... 😐😕😒

Some years ago, this guy I was really into and who I thought was incredibly deep told me sum'n. He said, "time does not define love." And I was like wow... that's so true. It rings true in this current place of my life; and it has made me hella anxious and vulnerable. I HATE being vulnerable. I'm nervous that if I tell someone who I truly feel about them, the feeling won't be reciprocated. This is when that motto comes into play: time does not define love. I feel like it's too soon... but in the same sense, I can't help how I feel. Legitimately, when I'm in... I'm all in. I know men move differently and feel differently from women.

However, I gotta get it out and say what I need to say. I'm too old to be playing games at the big age of 31. I'm scared and also agitated. Lol. Agitated because now everytime I talk to this person... I wanna say it and can't or I'm afraid of what his reaction will be. In hindsight, I'm proud of myself. Extremely proud of myself because this time last year... I wasn't able to be this open or honest. That goes for being vulnerable as well. So, with that being said and how Tommy from the Rugrats would say: "A baby's gotta do, what a baby gotsta do." Pray my strenf. In my head I swear I'ma thug... but my heart says otherwise. love. all ways. always.

POM: (4/1/2020)

April 1st. It's only right that you play Bone-Thugs-N-Harmony today. 🙊 it's still early in the year but these months have been moving fast. Today I had an epiphany. I am extremely proud of myself. I've seen hella growth within the last 6 months. Like I always say, day by day is the motto. Sometimes, if not often, I don't give God enough praise or talk to him as much as I should. I am doing better with that and in the midst, always staying grateful and humble. There's literally so much going on in the world at the moment that it's hard to keep up. I'm not gonna lie tho... my anxiety is on 1,000,000. Mainly over things I can't control. I just want there to be some type of normalcy again. It looks like spring is pretty much cancelled, as well as summer. All I can do is work, sleep, eat, pray and repeat. *not necessarily in that order*

The unknown/uncertainty is a scary place to be. But, all we can do is continue to take life day by day. LITERALLY. This too shall pass. The world is in a gray area... there's no black and white right now. However, this is just a brief moment for me to realize how far I've come emotionally and mentally... just overall me being proud of myself. We gotta check in on ourselves every now and then. Still alotta growth happening, as it should. Pray for peace. Pray for strength. Pray for faith. Pray for health. Pray for discernment. Pray for healing. love. live life. proceed. progress.

719: (4/4/20)

t's interesting how you think life is supposed to go. I'm 31, and don't have kids. Idk if I'll ever have kids. A part of me wants to have them and the other part is terrified of being a parent. I'd like to have at least one so I can have a legacy and so I can say, 'Go get me the remote!" Not only that, but also to break generational curses/cycles. When I was younger, I'd say "I don't want no kids!!!!" I've never been a kid person. Lol. But as you get older of course your perspective changes. With that being said, I have nephews and nieces... who I never get to see. Partially my fault and partially because the relationship was never initiated. Tbh, I don't have a relationship with any of my siblings... and it hurts. That's a big reason why I cherish my friends so much.

When I was in high school my family all lived in the same house. (My mom, sis & her kids and my grandmother). My sister had back to back kids while I was in high school. I helped take care of them. Those were my babies. ESP my oldest nephew cuz he was my first baby boy. I miss him being small. He used to wait on me to get outta school. Now he's 16. ☹ I've always wanted to be aunt that I never had. I wanted to show them things that I had been shown. Show them a different side of life. When they're not your own, it's hard to do. I learned the hard way that there's a thin line between parent and family member.

Long story short, my relationship with my sister become heavily strained because of her 'The world owes me everything' attitude. With that, meant me not dealing with her... I couldn't see my babies. I've always done for them. I'm the only aunt that has ever really came around, took them out, and just been there. But let my big headed sister tell it... I've never done anything. I just stopped coming around all together. Now that they're teenagers... it's almost like I have to start all over again. In the back of mind, I said I would lowkey wait until they got older to establish a relationship with them. So that they can see me for who I really am and not their mother's idea of me. I'm not gon lie... I'm in my world all the time. I rarely talk to my family... unless it's my parents or close friends. I don't have a relationship with any of my aunts, uncles, or cousins. How fucking sad is that??? Smh. It is what it is. I guess I'm feeling some type of way because today is my niece's birthday. She's turning 14. I feel so old. My babies are no longer babies. They're bad ass teenagers. 🙃 at the end of the day... I just hope we can establish a great relationship and they end up being great people.

Night Skies: (4/29/20)

Wow. I'm at work...sitting on the dock, waiting for my last break and looking forward to going home. I literally just had an epiphany. I was randomly thinking about how my mom was staying with me for 3 months last year. While I was thinking about this... I was like yoooooooooooo!!! I've literally been holding it down for myself. Through my ups and downs... I have shown up for myself, even when I didn't think I could. I believe this is this case, because most of the time all I've had is MYSELF. My struggle has definitely been one. Financially, mentally, and emotionally. Yet, I'm still STANDING. Wow. The smallest things I'm grateful for. 32 in about a month and I'm incredibly appreciative. Own car, own crib, decent (but annoying job), clothes on my back, food in my fridge, and some money in my bank account. Also, in the process of bettering my finances so I can become a homeowner. Is this what 30+ insight is? If so, I love it. Shoutout to me for legitimately holding it down even when things were hard, you wanted to give up/in and be nonexistent to the world. Life is about moments. In this moment, I am proud of me. We often forget about the trials and tribulations we went thru to get to our current destination. Wow. Thank you, God. Thank you, self. More blessings to come. More appreciation. More gratitude. More beauty. More lessons. More of my authentic self. love. all ways. always.

Whoa 'Der: (5/28/2020)

Life is interesting for sure. And God also has a funny sense of humor. Everyone knows (I think) that I'm asleep during the day because I work 3rd shift. For the past month or so I've been ordering way too many Amazon packages so I randomly get a knock on my door. Ironically today, I was half way woken up by the occasional knock. I received flowers. I knew they weren't from my boo. I looked for a card on the beautiful bouquet of flowers. I read the the message and I was tryna figure out who they were from. I put 2 and 2 together. I believe they're from a person that was once important to me. I still dunno how to feel about it. I'm appreciative of the sentiment. However, I'm not sure if this is an attempt to reconcile or what. I don't want to reconcile our relationship. I don't want to reconnect with someone that blatantly disrespected, violated, and overall has so no respect for myself, my environment, and even my mental health. I would however like to have a conversation... to get ALL of my feelings out in the most adult/mature way possible. I know that most likely I'll never get a real apology. The timing is interesting. I don't wanna overthink the situation. But in my mind... I'm thinking like, I got flowers... so what? What I'd like is an apology for the fuckery you did. Not only that, I would like for you to OWN what you did, acknowledge what you did, how it made me feel etc. I'm a grown woman. I can own my shit. I know who I am. I can effectively apologize. I can't say the same for this person. I know I'll never get an apology or a conversation that's woman to woman. At the moment, I can't say I fully forgive her. I need more time. Like I said, I appreciate the sentiment but that's about it. 👻I'll always have love for you. I can never forget you. I pray that you can heal how you need to. And I also pray that God puts it on my heart to fully forgive you... but more so for myself. Thank you for teaching me certain lessons that I carry til this day. You should take heed and practice what you preach. love. all ways. always.

Lemonade: (5/28/2020)

I should definitely be asleep because I have to work tonite. But, unfortunately I'm wide awake and hungry. Just laying in bed but I decided to go to my 'vibe room'. Playing one of my favorite albums by SiR. As always I have epiphanies. Alotta people know my family is pure dysfunctional. Many years ago I made the decision to just not be bothered and to stay in my lane. Life is much easier when you choose to put yourself first. And while it is easier, many would say it is selfish. Is it wrong of me to not wanna be bothered? Is it wrong of me to not wanna be involved with foolishness and chaos? Is it wrong of me to not wanna be wrapped in negativity? Just because they're so-called 'family'....

I know I'm not too good because they're a part of me. I am them. They helped raised me. Sometimes I feel like I have put myself in the 'too good' lane subconsciously. I hopped on social media to see that my sister has been released from jail. And I'm just like oh she's out after a couple of months. Realistically she needs to be in there and stay longer than 2-3 months. But I know her kids need her. If anything I feel bad for them because they haven't had stability in some years. It's always some drama going on with their mama. I'm not too good. But I have no desire to deal with family. I legit feel guilty. I guess that's because many years ago... I decided to put myself and my peace FIRST. I worry about me and me only. Everyone has their own shit they have to deal with. I guess this is mine. 👻 I want better for myself. I wish they did too. We all have to deal with life and the cards we're left to play. I may not have the best cards, nor the best odds. However... I'm doing my damnest to win the game. If I don't win.... just know I'll have a helluva comeback. love. all ways. always.

143: (6/4/2020)

To be genuine, faithful, loyal, and always be 100 these days is damn near impossible. I classify myself as being a solid individual. I always do what's asked of me, even when I don't want to. I always show up for people. With everything I do,

I'm solid and I love that about me. It's rare that you find someone on the same wavelength. One person that is the epitome of that is my father. I'm pretty sure that's where I get it from. He's a man of his word. So much that, he's taught me that all you have is your word. Some years ago, he told me... "One day you're gonna want a man like me. "When he said it, I was like "ewwww, what?!?! I don't wanna man like YOU."And lemme tell you... I couldn't have been more wrong. I want someone exactly like him. My dad is old school and ALWAYS keeps it 💯. He's never lied to me. He's ALWAYS come through when I need him x 10. He's SOLID. That's what I've wanted for a very long time. Now I have it... and I'm just in awe. He reminds me so much of my father that it's scary. It doesn't take a lot to appease me. But, I appreciate him so much. He's hardworking, giving, funny, loveable, honest (sometimes too honest) and most importantly SOLID. SOLID isn't a word that is used to often these days, but, I wanna bring it back. For so long I used to think something was/is wrong with me because I'm too hard on the outside. I'm too mean or I'm not dysfunctional enough. I've always been in my own lane, which is weird for most men. Because they like women that have nothing to offer, hella drama, or are thot pockets; that's the reality of it. So in this present time... I'm grateful and always appreciative for the gift of being solid AND it being reciprocated by someone I care about. It's an amazing feeling and I definitely don't take it for granted. I wish we had more men in the world like this, specifically black men. However, I'll admire my significant other, my father and the other great men in my life that exhibit the same qualities. You all are appreciated... in more ways than one.

love. all ways. always.

Summa Tings: (6/30/2020)

Life. It sure has a way of humbling you. I'm a witness. So many things I'm realizing these days. One is that life is precious and it is to be lived the way that you want it to; as long as it's legal and you aren't hurting anyone. Secondly, time waits for NO ONE. Thirdly, if you want something bad enough, 🗣YOU WILL MAKE IT HAPPEN. That's where I am right now. I've been talking about it and fantasizing about it for years. It's time to stop bs'n and make my dream come a reality. I'm actually excited now that I have a plan in motion. I know it will be far from easy, but I know ((or at least hope) it'll be worth it in the end. 32 feels really grown up to me. Idk why, lol. I still lowkey look like a baby in the face but I'm an adult. 🤦 I never quite had a plan for my life or where exactly I wanted to go. I've just always wanted stability. A strong yearning for it. I haven't had it throughout my adulthood. I've stayed on the struggle bus tryna maintain because I've had to live in survival mode. It's no fault of my own. Life mostly happens to us and as cliché as it may sound, it's all about how we react. And of course everyone's journey is different. I've had hella good things happen, as well as bad... but I've done my best to not live by that. I don't want the good things to define me, nor the bad. I'm just finding my way. I'm still striving for happiness, love, peace, and security within myself. Slowly but surely I'm curating the life I want. It's all a process. Not so much about the right now, but more so about the 'end game.' What is that you want out of life? Are you happy? What are you working towards? Questions I've been asking myself lately. I'm getting older and the days keep rolling by, which turn into weeks, months, and years. I want something magnificent and magical to show for myself. I don't wanna be miserable, regretful, and bitter when I'm 40+. That's a terrible way to live. My spirit and soul are so much bigger than that. I want all the happiness, peace, and love my heart can hold. I not only want that, I deserve it. We all do. love. all ways. always.

Authenticity: (7/8/2020)

Have you ever wondered what people see in you? Why they talk to you? What is so interesting about your personality? What do they find intriguing? I have, quite often. Not so much when I was younger, but definitely the last 10 years. I've always stayed in my lane and stayed true to myself. Genuine is what one quality that I love about myself. Maybe that's why some folks are so engaged by me. My sister once said that maybe my purpose in life is to remind people that are acting unloved that they ARE loved and still valuable. I have the worst resting bitch face, but I am as cool as an ice cube. 🏙️ I honestly dunno what is about me that causes people to just come up to me and start randomly talking but clearly, it's something about my energy. I'm not gonna lie...it's hard to keep a good energy/spirit about yourself. You have to keep yourself in check often. Trust and believe, that everyday isn't peaches and cream. But, you gotta choose to be the best version of yourself... even when you don't feel like it. I've met alotta dope people so far in my 32 years. And yet, I'm one the dopest people I've met. I'm still meeting ME. It's a lifelong journey. Things to think about....

I'll never be quite sure what people see when they talk to me through their own lenses. In hindsight, it's not meant for me to know. I'll just keep being Sunny & being my authentic self.

love. all ways. always.

Carl Thomas: (7/12/2020)

I hate being vulnerable. Like... I fucking HATE being vulnerable; which is also the reason why I've had a hard exterior for many years. Currently in my box o' feelz and that's not a place for anyone to be. My feelings are hurt, but, it's my fault. I wish I would've never said anything. Clearly the feeling was so strong, I just had to say sum'n. In that moment, it felt like my heart was gonna burst. I know I'm not being rejected... but in this present moment... I definitely feel like it. I never mean to pressure someone. In my mind certain things aren't that big of a deal. I feel like if I say I love you. 🙊 I MEAN THAT SHIT. There's no doubt in my mind. For someone to actively show me on a daily basis that they care... I know that they love me. I know they do. Because if they didn't... they wouldn't do half the shit they do. I just wanna hear it. I've put my heart and my ego on the line to say... 'hey, I love you and I'm in love with you.' I don't say that just because...I know that sometimes, if not often... it takes the opposite sex awhile to say the 3 words. I know it means that they don't care for me any less. And, I also respect that fact that they want to wait until they for sure know deep down in their heart. I've realized tho... I'm the opposite. If I say, I love you... I wanna hear it back!!! It sucks. But, I HAVE to respect what he has said, because I respect him as a man and I care deeply for him. Everyone knows I overthink everything. This shouldn't be that big of a deal, but it is. In this moment... IT IS. I can't help how I feel. I'm doing my best not to overthink/over analyze but it's hard. I just wish I never would've said anything. But, I feel how I feel. Even if it's not necessarily reciprocated how I want it to be. Growth... it hurts. But, we gotta go through it, to go through it...love. all ways. always.

143x2: (9/8/2020)

Love. A lot of people use it loosely these days. Love is an emotion to be felt in an unconditional manner with no stipulations. If I have ever said,'I love you' to someone, I genuinely mean it. I always say that you could meet someone yesterday and love them today like you've known them your whole life. I know because I've felt it more times than once in my life. At my big age of 32, we have no time to play games. NONE. More women are going after what they want in life. Not so much women, but EVERYONE. Life is precious. 2020 has been kicking ass and taking names. And with that being said, I don't have time for the Tom foolery that folks are on.

But, on the flip side of that... I've also learned a major lesson this year. Which is to: 🧏🏽‍♀️ USE YOUR WORDS. I'm not a mind reader and I'm definitely not going to attempt to do so or read between the lines. We're too grown!!! Mature people communicate effectively and that's a hard lesson I had to learn. But, I'm extremely glad that I did. How does someone know how you feel, unless you tell them? You hurt me. That made me upset. I don't like that. All examples (not good examples) of USING YOUR WORDS. This weekend I had to put my big girl drawz on and take my own advice. It was definitely a conversation that was uncomfortable for me to have, but it needed to be said. I did my best to be patient, understanding, with the intent of a strong listening ear. I can sometimes come off as an asshole when I'm tryna get my point across, but in that moment, I HAD to be vulnerable. And needless to say, I'm glad I was able to break down a wall and get what I needed. I'm still processing. Like WOW... do you see what can happen when you communicate effectively? We don't know, unless we ask. I'm proud of myself. But, I'm also kind of nervous. This isn't a place I've been before so I'm taking it seriously and lightly at the same time. I now have someone's heart in my hands... and it's a big deal. He trusts me enough to love him unconditionally through it all. I'm honest enough to say I don't wanna fuck anything up or have him do the same. But, it's life. No one is perfect. All we can do is give our best and USE OUR WORDS effectively. 143. love. all ways. always.

In real life tho: (9/30/2020)

In real life tho... (one of my favorite sayings) ...
I'm struggling at the moment. My anxiety is kicking my ass. The balance between being in the present and being overly focused on the future is heavy on my mind. My mouth is dry, thoughts are everywhere, and I'm overthinking the scattered thoughts in my brain. Not sure if it's from legit my anxiety or the 2 Pepsi's I drank... or if it's a combination of both. Some days are better than others, and other times it's a moment like this. Lil Duval once tweeted to sum'n like "People really like finding stuff to worry/stress about." I think that's true to a certain extent. I legit can't help it. Even on medication... it's a struggle. Pretty much all is well in my life... I honestly cannot complain. On the flip side... I am overwhelmed mentally and emotionally. I'm doing my best not to let it take over. I keep telling myself to just breathe and think of other positive thoughts, I can't. All that takes over is how exhausted/depleted of energy I am, how much I shouldn't be sleeping, the to do list I need to make, the guilt of not staying for the constant overtime of my job, and how much I desperately want to just disappear for a while. In real life tho, none of this matters. Still gotta put on a somewhat happy smile and go about life.

Some people say that I have a certain calm & peaceful energy about myself; which I can appreciate the sentiment. But, if they only knew the turmoil I go through internally on a daily basis. I wouldn't wish this on anyone. I've always had anxiety. ALWAYS. However, as I've gotten older... it has become 10x worse. At times it almost feels paralyzing to my spirit... because I know it's not normal. Le sigh.

BJJ (11/20/2020)

And so, it starts....

21 days which is equivalent to 3 weeks. It will have been a year. A year that I have been in a committed relationship with my significant other. I still can't believe it. The fact that I still like him, even when he gets on my nerves. That speaks volumes. Because I don't like people and my tolerance for stupidity/ignorance/ and other negativity is little to none. Throughout my life... adulthood I guess... I've been told that I have a wall up and I can come off as aggressive. I've always had a good head on my shoulders, a 'go getta' mentality, independent as hell, and just stayed in my lane. For a long time I thought that something was wrong with me or I would be single forever. I'm different. I'm not your average lady. I'm open minded and I do my best to see things from all angles and perspectives.

Some men that I've come across couldn't understand why I had been single for so long OR why I'm not being pursued as often as they thought I should. It came to my attention that I'm too normal for most men. I don't have any drama. No kids. No craziness. Job, my own crib, and own car? That's too much normalcy for a guy these days. The funny thing is I'm an introvert so I'm overwhelmingly fine with being by myself. With that being said, I don't let just anyone into my space or my life; and many don't understand that or don't want to understand. I don't want anyone in my life who can't match me, or not bring (if not more) to the table. I've always known my worth. I know that I'm an amazing woman. Smart, goal oriented, a big heart, genuine, and loving. I had just been waiting on the right one, who didn't necessarily have an ulterior motive or was on certified bullshit.

And here I am a year later happy and in love. Yes, I am still in disbelief. If you wanna make God laugh, tell HIM your plans. Life is ironic as hell. When you're so used to things going opposite, hella negative situations, and constant rejections... you begin to think you don't deserve happiness. You don't think it'll ever come, so you just become content with yourself and friends. Those who I love, love me back. I was cool with that. But deep down, I've always yearned for me. Now I have it and it's a scary but, yet beautiful place to be.

This is when self-sabotage comes into play... because sub consciously we feel we aren't worthy. OR we think something is gonna go wrong, even though everything is going right. To be real, I'm terrified. What if this is everything I imagined? What if I get dropped like a bad habit? What if? 🤦🏾‍♀️ WHAT IF!!! What if we both love each other so deeply that we find our way thru life together? What if? When I say my anxiety is on 1,000,000... that's an understatement. Neither one of us is perfect but we balance each other out. This year has been nothing but growth. We're growing together. Communicating effectively. Laughing endlessly. And whole heartedly supporting each other. This shit is scary. Of course every day isn't peaches and cream but we make it work. I'm honest enough to say I'm afraid that this thing will work and will go the distance. For someone that's been single the majority of her adulthood, it's a big deal. I guess that's why I stay in disbelief that I've been in a relationship almost a whole year with no real problems. Shit happens, but, it's great to know that I have someone to go through it with. Life is hard enough on a daily basis, so we all need at least one person to help us stay soft when obstacles are thrown at us. I'm not sure what the future holds for us, but I'm grateful for the time and moments we've shared thus far. Love people while you have them. Love unconditionally. Love loud. Love fearlessly. Love whole heartedly. love. all ways. always.

Lesss Be Real: (12/14/2020)

Let's be real. I normally hate the holidays. It's just another day to me. Because my family dynamic is so jacked up, I typically feel some type of way especially on Thanksgiving and Christmas. I have always wanted to change my feelings about it. But, I knew it wouldn't change until I had a family of my own or I started my own traditions. This year is completely different and I am thankful for that. I am actually excited. I have been with my significant other a year, so I am looking forward to spending time with him and his kids. I've never been in this space. I can't lie, the last 10 years have been lonely, somewhat miserable, and definitely disheartening. That's why I just chalk it up as another day and do my best not to think about it. Everyone normally has their own thing going on... and I just don't want to be bothered. I used to be sad just thinking about it, until I became numb. I used to be so hurt that my so called, "family" would only want to get together on the holidays or if someone was sick/in the hospital. We never contact each other throughout the calendar year, but now you want me to fake the funk and act like I'm happy to see you for a day? Nahhh, I'll pass. With that being said, I appreciate my friends so much more. My friends are my family. And this year I am a part of a new family and tbh it feels really good. The only thing that really sucks is I have to work, so I can't fully enjoy the day how I want to; but I am happy to be included and feel loved in the same way. I don't think I've ever felt like this.I'm just happy to start new beginnings, even if it's not what I envisioned... and that's the best part of all. love. all ways. always.

Big Age: (2/27/2021)

Peace, love, and souuuullllll. This is a random thought: but, for the most part I love the older people I work with. Sometimes they're a little messy with gossip but they always drop major gems. For some reason I've always resonated with older people, and that's probably why everyone calls me old. I love my blankets, I don't mind going to bed early, and just my overall demeanor. 😂🏚️ I love the fact that no matter how old they are, they see the potential in me... they see I'm a good person with a good head on my shoulders. That's always made me feel so good about myself. Cuz you know old(er) people LOVE to talk shit about the younger generation. Recently I started going to the gym after YEARS of needing it. I'm not gonna lie, it feels good to be in this space. Knowing that I am actively & diligently working on becoming the best version of myself. It's funny tho, all the old heads I talk to are like... "Just keep going, don't give up. You're young. Go ahead and make it happen." To hear them say I'm young makes me subconsciously laugh. Technically I am. At 32, I am still young. Unfortunately society dictates otherwise. My dad will be 68 in a couple of months & all he ever says is "Keep on living. Hopefully you make it to this age." And he's right. If not often, we think that once we hit our 30s that we're officially old. However, that couldn't be more further from the truth. Luckily, both my parents have good genes & I look like I'm still in my 20s. 🪤 Age is definitely is a stigma & it's really a mindset. I'm not even gonna lie, 32 has been good to me. I've actually enjoyed it. While in your 30s, alotta things make more sense and it's more of... 'I ain't got time for the bullshit and it is what it is' type of mindset. And I fully support it. It's a lot smoother, more awareness of self, & accepting things for what they are & not what you want them to be. Like my Pops said, 'Keep on living.' Everyday ain't peaches and cream, but, gotta keep on moving regardless of what's happening. In this moment, I'm grateful to be the big age of 32. Cuz people are dying now more than ever, especially in this pandemic. Slow & steady on this health journey. I'm not just tryna be summa time fine at 32, but the rest of my life. I appreciate everyone who's keeping me encouraged, supported, & loved on. You know what? It's love.... all ways, always.

ALB: (4/21/21)

It's been 4 days since you've been gone and I still can't wrap my mind around it. I always knew this day would come, but in the back of my mind I've always thought you were invincible... cuz you are high key a superhero. I can't fathom all of the things you went thru... all of the things you witnessed in your 89 years. You can never really prepare yourself for death... it just comes and unfortunately it's a natural part of life. I'm not necessarily thinking of negative stories of you and I. I'm moreso thinking about how I lost my grandmother. The woman that helped raised me. All the images that come to mind are from 4 days ago. Your body laying there and being ice cold when I gave you a kiss on the forehead. Anne Laura is and was a beast. Very complicated woman who definitely had a mean streak. But, I think that comes from the era she grew up in. Parents/grandparents often do the best they can with what they're given. I loved hearing her talk about my granddaddy and all of her side hustles back in the day. How she wanted all of us to be well off and doing good in life. This wave of grief/sadness is overwhelming to the point that it makes me numb. I have alotta feelings. Not really ill feelings but just the disbelief that she's gone. I wish that I would've went to see her more. But I just couldn't see her in such an ailing/fragile state. It hurt my soul to see her like that. I'll forever miss her saying, "Well hey there Trice. I'm happy to see you." Whenever I would pop up on her. Seeing her on that gurney is haunting me. I pray that her soul is in heaven. I'm beyond sad. No one anything says to me will make me feel better. My last living grandparent is gone. We all knew it was a matter of time. Years ago, I remember you talking about it and your funeral arrangements. I would tune you out cuz I didn't want to think about you dying. And yet, here we are. I have pretty good memories of you. Me taking you to the doctor, grocery store, our random phone calls. Also when I was little you taking me to Burger King and letting me get a whopper with cheese (cuz I couldn't have cheese when I was younger. 🙁☹). All the times I got in trouble and you told my mama don't mess with me.😊 you always asking me if I've eaten when I'd pop up at your house. The fact that you always asked if I had a boyfriend, which will forever be hilarious to me cuz you loved to gossip. Anne Laura, I'm hurting right now. But I know you've been hurting for YEARS. That alone doesn't ease my pain. There are so many things to say, but none of it really matters because I can't tell you. My 4'11 little lady. Whew...Not gonna say goodbye but more of a 'see ya later.' I know you're watching over me & I hear you saying not to be sad & to stop crying but I can't help it. It's been rough going thru everyday life the last 4 days. All I can think of is you being gone. You loved us so hard. You went hard for everybody. Even when you were being crazy. It's in our DNA to be strong. Although I can't be strong enough to deal with this but I'll do my best for you.

Missin' U: (4/26/2021)

It's been a week since you've been gone and I'm still in disbelief. I hate feeling like this. A piece of me is gone & it's never coming back. I get why people say, "My condolences, or I'm sorry for your loss." doesn't mean anything. I totally understand now. Those sentiments do not make me feel any better, it still makes me want to burst out in tears. Your memorial is coming up & I'm dreading it. Not ready to say goodbye. Another part of me is ready, just so I can properly grieve how I need to. Grieving/mourning feels A LOT like depression, & that's not a place I want to be. For the longest time it's been just us... me, my mom, my gma, & my sister. Now you're gone & idk what to do or how to feel. They say grief is ongoing & everyone deals with it differently. It is definitely a large blow to me personally. I will say that today has been the easiest day of the week. I've been a little bit more talkative & cool to be around. I know the pain of you being gone will never go away but hopefully it gets easier. I keep looking at your pictures thinking man you were mean, but also super sweet (when you wanted it to be, lol). You were indeed a sour patch kid. You loved us to the best of of your ability. Sometimes you went all the way left, but I believe your heart was in the right place. I'm thankful for the prayers from people that are close to me. Day by day, it gets slightly easier. love. all ways. always.

Angel Hands: (5/27/2021)

I've had alotta idle time while working this morning, which means I've been thinking. The last week or so has been turmoil for me, more so mentally and emotionally. I suppose physically too, because my body has been hurting nonstop. When my body hurts like this it's stress and anxiety. Today is the first morning in about 2 weeks that I kinda feel okay. I know that's only from God and the people in my life that are genuinely praying for me. I need it. Some days are better than others. The last month has been extremely difficult. One of my good friend's pointed out that I'm currently dealing with trauma, which that's actually accurate af. I lost my grandmother due to bladder cancer, I have disheartening images of her on a gurney, tryna be there/support my mom… all while my sibling is being an ignorant jack ass on social media AND in real life. So yes, it's been a doozy. I don't wanna trip anymore… my birthday is coming up in 6 days and I don't wanna go into 33 being incredibly depressed. I wanna get back into some type of normalcy. I suppose I should continue taking my own advice, "day by day." I've realized that I have to be gentle with myself and offer myself grace, considering that everything is affecting me at the moment. I hate when someone asks me, "Are you ok?" I REALLY wanna say,

"🗣 NO NIGGA, I'm not okay… I'm fucking depressed… stop talking to me." But I can't…

That's why I've been doing my best to reach out to my friends that know me well. Because they know (for the most part) what patterns are, especially when I shut down. I honestly hate shutting down, because my caring bone goes away. I ignore texts, phone calls, and any other type of communication. Trust me, it's not intentional… it's how I cope. And unfortunately, when I shut down… it does more harm than good. But when you're in that deep dark hole of depression… you literally want to be left alone. You feel numb, hopeless, discouraged, disconnected and overwhelmingly sad. It's a hard to bounce back. So not only am I dealing with depression & anxiety… but I have to adult daily too??? LISSSSEEEENNNN. I don't have time. I have too many goals to accomplish this year for the nonsense. But, remember the word GRACE? Gotta give myself enough grace and space (hey, that rhymes ☺) to grieve how I need to and feel how I need to, without being too hard on myself or feeling guilty. It's just hella emotions tied into one, so forgive me if I'm rambling. Moral of the story is… today… this morning… I feel God's grace and some type of peace. I am humbly grateful that my inner circle is praying for me, cuz I desperately need it. My angels are looking over me. I know they are cuz I feel it. It's still hard to cope, but I'm making it thru. If you read this, I'm still asking for prayer/positive thoughts/good energy. I'm just thankful that today is better than what it has been…

Low & Behold: (8/14/2021)

I hate it when people say calm down and don't overthink! How? HOW? questions that need answers. Today I realized that overthinking is definitely a form of self-sabotage. And I do not know how to turn this off. Cuz once it starts, ain't no going back. It's scary. My mind constantly racing, as well as my heart. That happens and the most drastic decision happens, based on the situation going on. For me there is no gray area. Strictly black and white. There is no alternative or no 'meeting halfway' or compromise. My therapist told me once to entertain the gray. I did and it wasn't too bad. But now I'm back to square one and it sux. At the moment I'm not sure how to confirm if it's God's voice or my ability to self-sabotage. I honestly don't know how to differentiate the two. My OG told me to pray about until God reveals what to do next. BUTTTTT, I don't have the words to say. It's extremely weird being in this place. I'm all for growth but this shit hurts. Growth… (if you're up for the challenge), is a doozy. So many things I'm learning & unlearning, unpacking my baggage while simultaneously being in a relationship. I legitimately feel crazy. Crazy because it seems like almost every two weeks, I'm in my thoughts or box o feelz. While fighting through not shutting down…. maybe God is tryna tell me sum'n. I am all over the place. But, I'm beginning to think I'm the problem. What I often feel seems/sounds valid, until I say it aloud or vent to someone. Then overthinking comes into play. Yes, you can tell me all day long to calm down or say, "It's not that deep." OH, but it is! Everything and I do mean EVERYTHING I feel is… INTENSE. I hate it. I hate that I can't just let things roll off my back. I hate that after a conversation with someone, I think of all the things I said or shouldn't say. I hate the fact that I always wonder what people think about me and it's none of my concern. I hate the fact that I'm even writing these words at the moment. You see? So, it's a lot… for me. Overthinking is not something I ever intended to do. It takes you towards a downward spiral that leads to even more severe anxiety and depression. Anxiety in itself is crippling, and add overthinking to the mix? Lordt have mercy. I'm doing my best to cope and take things day by day, but I can't. My anxiety is overwhelming at the moment. I can recognize & acknowledge where I am in life… emotionally & mentally. I kinda feel like I'm drowning in my own misery and I'm the only person that can save me. As I've gotten older, I really see how your mental health can affect you. Dealing with depression, severe anxiety doesn't define me and I'll never let it. However, it's definitely plays a major role in my life on the daily. I'm not claiming anything negative, letting the Devil have his way, or putting it into the universe. I'm stating FACTS. Despite me currently feeling like this... I am really proud of myself. Granted I'm still working on myself a lot, I've come a long way... and still a long way to go. I can't wait to get my ass back in therapy. Hopefully REALLY REALLY soon. It helped me work out some issues within myself and other people. It's that time again. I know what I deserve. And I know it starts with me. I know I can't receive my blessings if I'm self-sabotaging. God knows it too... that's prolly why it's so intense in my spirit. He be KNOWIN'. lol. I'm glad I got this off my chest. I feel just a tad bit lighter...love. all ways. always.

516: (8/15/2021)

Functioning. It is crazy to me how life goes on while you're internally going thru turmoil. The world is just passing you by, while you want to just disappear. I've always believed I am different. In every sense in the word. I've always felt different and moved different. Different, how? I'm not sure. As I got older I realized I was an outcast and I always wanted to be left alone, because I felt like no one understood me. I just wanted to get away from everything… even in high school. Years later it was brought to my attention that it's called depression. And with that, I've always been worried and tend to overthink A LOT, which in fact is anxiety. Realistically, I've been dealing with these issues my whole life. They're just weren't talked about or made of importance until about 8-10 years ago. The fact that I've been FUNCTIONING for YEARS on end is amazing. I've always suppressed my feelings of inadequacy, doubt, rejection, and feeling unloved. Dealing with all of this and being in survival mode is enough to take anyone past their lowest point. But, it is ongoing. It is literally…. LITERALLY a spiritual/emotional/mental warfare inside of me. How is it that I know what God says & what HE has done for me, but I'm still having thoughts of death? That is so unbelievably selfish of me. It's a fine line. God knows there's a reason why I'm on this earth. I'm not sure what it is, but I pray HE reveals it to me sooner than later. Every 3-6 months I go thru this phase where I doubt everything; and it feels like I'm constantly asking myself what's my point in being here?

Last night while I was headed to work… I was fighting back tears. I kept having really negative thoughts. Once I got on the highway I literally had to keep saying, "Devil get up offa me." I knew that's who it is. It feels like a spiral… like a tornado of toxic ass emotions, numbness, and wanting to die. This shit ain't normal. Unfortunately, it is my reality. And some days are better than others. Constantly having to work thru your shit is so draining and painful….. BUTTTTTT… gotta keep working. The goal is to NOT let the devil win, heal, strengthen your faith, and keep working on YOU. Even though I am super sweet, genuine, cool, laidback, and chill? I'm suffering and it ain't all peaches and cream. However, I'm pushing though despite how I currently feel. Also know… functioning is HARD.

Whodini: (8/29/2021)

Frenz? How many us of have them? Frenz? The one we can depend on." And yes, I'm quoting Whodini lyrics. Lol. Man, it's been long ass night/morning. I hate it when it's slow motion at work, it makes the time DRAG by. Anyway. I've been thinking a lot about my friendships lately. One thing about me… my circle is small and I like it that way. I have a handful of friends that I really fuck with. So needless to say, I go UP and I show out. I really wish more people would show up for the ones they care about. I definitely do wayyy too much, but idk any other way. I just feel like, if you love someone and you KNOW for a fact that they're loyal to the soil…

Why wouldn't you want to go above and beyond? I'm not speaking just about monetary or things that are tangible. But moreso emotional, mental, and spiritual support. Granted, I am not always in the space to support them how I need to, but I damn sure do my best. Like, I really love my friends. I mean, I love them for who they are and what they represent in my life. My family are my friends. The dysfunction and chaos that I have to deal with my family. My friends do more than take up space. We get on each other's nerves, occasionally and curse each other out… but the love? That's so genuine and my actions prove it.

Being an empath… is hard. So when my friends go thru sum'n, so do I. I feel all of that energy, and it hurts. It hurts to know that my friend(s) are going through it; ESPECIALLY when I can do **anything about it. But, it's life. All I can continue to do is pray for them and hope they have** some type of peace. I've always done by best to rest those how I want to be treated, and for the most part it's worked out. Luckily for me, I learned years ago that just because you do right by people, that doesn't mean that they're going to do right by you. Feel me? Sometimes that's a hard lesson to learn. But, that's why I said my circle is small. Anything that I do is because I wanna see you happy/brighten your day or simply a 'just because' text to let you know I love you. That's me. I just wish that people would love on each more. It's so much fuckery going on in the world. I don't want any hate, ill will, or negativity in my heart or towards anyone. Who has that type of time? Life is short. I want anyone I care about to WIN.

It's weird tho… because when I typically go thru sum'n, so does someone I'm close to. This is just a reminder, that even if you're going through it. You're not alone. I hope you hear my positive thoughts and prayers, and know that I have hug waiting for you. Life is tough enough… but just know I got you for as long as I have breath in my body. love. all ways. always.

Ainee', Sha, Danielle, Morgan, Chyna, Bridgette, Dawn, DJ, Thomas, Cedric, Harold, and Mawa. This is for y'all.

Jus Chill: (9/22/2021)

amorously, I've learned to love/care so deeply, be more open/understanding and challenging myself emotionally. I've expanded boundaries and taken more accountability than ever. For a long time I didn't think this was possible. I didn't know think that I would ever feel love so deeply or find a companion that really GOT ME. And then, I found someone. My whole life shifted. Shifted for the better. It's been scary but I can honestly say that I've been better for the journey. In the beginning I didn't so much question a lot of things or emotions, because I was just happy. But now? I have to question everything because… I don't want to settle from me making someone else incredibly comfortable. That's a joy I have. To make people happy, comfortable etc. There are little things that eventually show up in big form. My feelings are crazy, but I know that they're valid. This is when I have to listen to my intuition AND God's voice. I'm sitting still and processing without the beast of overthinking/panicked.

I can't lie and say my anxiety isn't on overdrive but I'm handling things a lot better than I have in the past…(or at least I think I am)…One thing I've learned about myself is… despite me 'loving hard' and wanting things to work out for themselves… I can walk away. Yes, love will be there all ways. But in this season, it's time to get back to me… plant more seeds of self-love and continue to know what I'm worth.

Love. Life Live. Proceed. Progress: (9/26/2021)

I wish I could convey into words of how I feel at the moment. I feel like no matter how much I talk about it… no one really gets it. I've literally been in my bubble and staying to myself lately. My OG told me to sit still and listen to God's voice; which I've been doing my best to do so. I've been cool lately, but yesterday it hit me… probably the main reason why I didn't get too much sleep before work. I haven't been sad in a while, but today I feel all of it, every emotion. I guess I'm sad because I know what has to be done. I don't want to be single. I really don't. Tbh, everyone knows it's slim pickings outchea. I don't wanna date and get to know someone new. No desire, at all. 🪤 ⋮ I'm 33 years old with no children. Yes, the world is my oyster… however it currently doesn't feel like that. I want a family. I want someone that's going to return all the love I give and then some. What's crazy to me is…, I just realized it, but, in this particular situation…. I've literally given all that I have. In every sense of the word. I've been fighting myself for a while, but it's time to listen to my intuition. I'm hurt. I'm sad, I'm frustrated.

To know that I wanted to spend my life with someone, and now I'm choosing to be single? It's a weird space to be in. Extremely weird. Even tho my spirit is everywhere… this is the best choice at the moment. I've lost myself. I recognize this and I have to change it. Being self-aware sometimes sux, especially when you love yourself AND others love you enough to call out the bullshit that's happening. I will say that I'm proud of myself. For knowing when to walk away, especially when you know you have given all you have and then some. I've always been different and had a different type of heart, which is a major blessing. However, alotta people don't know what to do with it. I love hard and I never realized it until I got in this relationship.

At this point, I'm just tryna keep my peace and sanity without going into a downward spiral of depression. It's hard. Really hard, especially now that I have made an executive decision. I'm still a little unsure, but this discernment that I've been praying for is incredibly intense. And with that being said… if you read this, pray for your girl. These growing pains are a doozy…love. all ways. always.

Cold Hands, Warm Heart: (9/28/2021)

When your best isn't enough. What do you do? Give it to God. Or at least that what my mama said. I really be trippin' over life…

Like one minute you're cool and then BAM! 💥 the next minute your whole life changes in an instant. I think about my life a lot. What I mean to people, what they mean to me, my purpose, and everything I've been through this far. I've come an incredibly long way. To see my growth is amazing AND for other people to see/acknowledge my growth is amazing as well. Although these growing pains hurt, I'm in awe with myself.

I'm staying true to my word. I know what I'm worth and I don't want to settle. God built me different. Learning that I'm an empath makes so much more sense to me as I get older. After tapping into my vulnerability via therapy. AND being in a relationship… I've had to learn the sensitive spots of my heart, mind, and spirit. So with all that… I'm a sensitive hot mess mixed with empathy. I'm dealing with my own issues on top of feeling everyone else's emotions. It's crazy! I was today years old when I realized it. Imagine how heavy all of this feels on a daily basis. I've come to terms that solace, quietness, and sleep is how I manage. Sometimes I'll come home and won't turn on anything. I'll just sit in silence or even drive in silence. Not all the time, but it's becoming more often and I'm okay with it. In this moment I am doing alright. However, I know some days will be better than others. I also know that healing takes time. I've given so much of myself away in this particular relationship and that's not necessarily a bad thing. It has just taught me that I'm able to love. And although, I've given alotta myself to someone… that just means that I'm ready to love even harder the next go round. I just need to make sure that it's reciprocated how I need it to be. In the midst of my mind's chaos, I'm still processing… Life man… it be life'n…love. all ways. always.

PUSH: (9/29/2021)

Pray until something happens. Life has been a whirlwind of emotions the last 5-6 months. It has not been easy. Deaths, relationships, work, daily adulting, regular severe anxiety… the list goes on & on. But, I've persevered through it all. Almost a new month and I wanna go into October strong. I currently have peace. What's crazy to me is… like 3 people told me I look different this morning. Almost as if I have a different type of aura. One of those ppl said it looks like the weight has been lifted off my shoulders. And that's incredibly accurate. Granted, I'm tired because I'm still at work. BUT, I definitely have peace and I'm so very thankful. No idea how grateful. Typically when I go through something, my emotions are tying me down. I've been so mentally disconnected, frustrated, and just disappointed the last 3 months. So to come to work and my co-workers are telling me that I lost weight/slimmin' down, and that I have a certain glow? Baby, that's GOD. I literally had to PUSH through especially as of late. It is the little things. I just knew breaking up with a significant other after almost 2 years together would put me somewhere I didn't wanna be. However, it's the total opposite. I have peace knowing I did my best, loved as hard as could and was there to support him in any capacity. I hate that the split had to happen, but I've been fighting myself for way too long. So, God had been in my ear heavy and I FINALLY listened. I'm honestly happy. I'm relieved. I can go on with my life without being miserable. This lets me know everything will be alright.

🖤🖤🖤love. all ways. always.

Fox'n It: (1/4/2022)

It's 3 days into the new year. What I have accomplished this far? Not a damn thing. Being off from work has me looking like a confused fox. Not sure what to do. l was literally in bed all day. Only moved to use the bathroom and check the mail. Then my back decided that it wanted to start hurting. - side note: I don't appreciate random parts of my body hurting just cuz…especially at 33. 😐

Anyway. I've been in my head a lot. Doing my best to not think about last year and all that's happened to me and around me. Missing my granny heavily… I keep looking at her picture. Wishing I could pop up on her one more time or talk to her. It honestly feels like my life is empty or I'm lacking. Between the holiday season just ending, being single (by choice), and just overall wondering the next phase of my life will bring. Not gonna lie, I miss my ex. He was my best friend. I feel a massive void. I'm pretty sure it's a delayed reaction. When I first ended things… I felt super strong and empowered. Proud that I was able to put myself first and stand true to my wants, needs, and desires. And now? I'm still all of those things. But, all I can think about is the time invested, our conversations, and just having someone constantly there. It fucking sucks. Even though, it hits different… I know I made the best decision for me. I know it hit me differently because of the holidays and I'm sooooo glad it's over. Tbh, I gotta get back to me. I put him first for the majority of our relationship. As much as I want to entertain hoes and be reckless out here in these streets… that life ain't meant for me. I'm honest to say that. So it's time for discipline and sacrifice. Insanity: doing the same thing over and over again and expecting different results. I mean, we're all insane to a certain extent but something has to give.

A part of me is afraid. Afraid of success. Afraid to break out of this generational curse of struggling. Afraid to be the person that's destined for greatness. You can tell me all day long not to be afraid, but, I'm human.. I guess it's time to put up or shut up. I'm the type of person where if I think about something too long I won't do it. So I just gotta tap in… all aspects of my life. I'm too dope of person to settle for anything mediocre. However, with that comes a fine balance. Gotta give yourself time and grace. Another reason I'm afraid is because I feel like I'm running out of time. I know that's far from the truth, but I'm 33… I was just 25. ☹ regardless I gotta figure it out and not let my past dictate my future. Easier said than done…love. all ways. always.

Tell It All: (1/21/22)

When we're children, we have all type of dreams. Sometimes our dreams stay the same and sometimes they change. Or maybe your parents are trying to live thru you and they push their dreams onto you. Either way it goes, things change. When I was like 8 or 9, I got my first journal for Christmas, which was low key life changing. In middle school I figured out that I liked to write and enjoy creative things. I thought that I wanted to be a director, producer, or be in some type of field of journalism. In high school it was on and poppin! That's when I was getting the composition notebooks and started writing poetry. I would occasionally share with friends, and think that it was so deep. 😊 but in reality, I wasn't talking about anything. Eventually I stopped writing because I felt like my stuff was whack. I went onto experiment in different industries of work. I've literally done a little bit of everything. But, at the end of the day I've always had a passion for English. I once took an Etymology class and it was one of the best things I've ever done. I love using big words, especially when I want to prove a point or sound super smart. Lol. When I was younger I always felt misunderstood. It was like no one cared what I had to say. Or I didn't have enough courage to speak up for myself. Writing is everything to me. You can take what you want from my words. Hopefully the person reading my work will be able to relate. It makes me feel free. Because I suffer from anxiety/depression… my mind is constantly on a hamster wheel and my thoughts just keep going around and around. It's quite maddening and frustrating. When that happens, I choose to write. I saw this quote on Twitter that said, "Write for your life." And it couldn't have been said better. Writing has saved my life on many occasions. When I was in college, one of my mentors asked me when I was going to start writing again. I said I don't have anything to say. She told me, "You always have something to say. You're a writer and it's always going to be in you." She was absolutely correct. When someone reads my work and can relate? Omg… my heart explodes and makes me feel so good. Writing is cathartic, as well as my therapy. Even if no one else reads my work, I'm cool with that. I do it for me. At the end of the day I know my weapon, which is my pen. And once I write my thoughts down? I'm lethal. love. all ways. always.

Gimme Room: (1/30/2022)

Loner life. For as long as I can remember, I've always been to myself and by myself. I'm not sure what that reason is. I do remember not having too many friends & definitely being socially awkward for the majority of my childhood up until about 10 years ago. I've always been quiet and shy. Never said what was on my mind until I got in my 30s. I often wish I would've stood up for myself more. But, it's cool. Because now I'm at the age that I am… idgaf and I'll just wish you a blessed/prosperous life, and go about my way. 👻 what's crazy is… I think my loner and introvert ways are partially because I was a latch key kid. When your mom has to work and doesn't have a baby sitter? The protocol is: don't answer the door, call me at work if it's an emergency, and there's food in the fridge. And when I come home yo chores better be done or you're on punishment. It was really easy to follow the protocol. But in hindsight, that's probably a reason why I have severe anxiety now. I've always had a worried/stressed nature about myself. Lol. Waiting for your parent to get home, you're by yourself, and it's dark as hell outside? My inner child is cringing at the thought.. As an adult, I've tapped into the latch key kid theory. I don't deal with a lot of ppl. I don't answer the door unless invited. I choose who and what is allowed in my space. Growing up, my sister always had me as her tagalong. My mama made sure of it. Being 8 years older than me had its perks. But once she became 21+, it was a wrap. She was out here doing hoodrat shenanigans, while I was tryna figure out how to be a socially awkward teenager. Once she left the house, my mom was always at work and my grandma at home watching her stories… all I had was loneliness, SpongeBob and 106 & Park. (Real ones know 🫰). In hindsight and without being in therapy, I've realized that part of my life has affected me. I'm so used to being alone, that it's crazy. So for me to wanna kick it with you, your energy has to make me wanna be around you: BECAUSE my peace is everything. It's probably the reason that I get easily annoyed when I do get visitors. In my mind: I'm thinking, damn when are you going home? 😒🥴😏 I'd rather be alone in peace than be surrounded by constant chaos and drama. It has also affected my relationships as well. I have to really like/love you to be in my space, especially a long time if it's a long time. Constant time by yourself lowkey makes you a "no none sense" type of individual. You're ready to tell a mofo how you feel and how they got you fucked up. You know why? Because you don't need them! You're good by your damn self. But then again, it's lonely sometimes. However, you got options baby! For the bulk of my adulthood, I didn't understand folks that constantly had to be in someone's face or always have someone around them. Then it dawned on me... everyone is different. I can go out to eat, go to the movies, a concert or just chill at home by my damn self. Idk anything else other than my introvert ways. That's possibly because there hasn't been alotta folks that have constantly been around me. In my life, yes. But in my personal space, no. If I miss you or you're on my mind super heavy... I have no problem pulling up vice versus. Especially now that everything is so crazy. I don't get to see people or spend time. I blame it on the pandemic, being an introvert, and working all the time. I wouldn't say that alone time is necessarily a bad thing. For me, it works. It works for my peace of mind, sanity, and all the things that come with life, while you're tryna find yourself. S/o to all the latch key kids! Let us remember how the 90s were poppin and we are officially getting old.

The Ancestors: (2/1/2022)

I remember years back talking to my grandmother about when I was born. She said I was bright eyed and bushy tailed and was looking all over the room. I just smiled as she recalled me being born. From a young age, I've always been different. For some reason, I have always resonated with older people. Many say that I 'act old'. I used to be offended by it, but now I just embrace it. My mindset and demeanor isn't what it should be. Throughout my life and even now, I take the lessons that I've learned from older folks and do my best to apply them to real life. Maybe it's the stories they tell, or the constant encouragement that life ain't so bad. I need that. I need a constant reminder that I'm doing okay in life and it could always be worse. From the new generation… I'd say anyone younger than 25, hearing their conversations are cringe worthy. At work I hear them all the time and I literally have to walk away. The arrogance, ignorance, and overall agitation that I feel. Different type of spirit is what I am. I feel like I have knowledge to pass to others. In a sense I also feel like, depending on how a person grew up… the simplest things… they may not know how to do. For example, when I got my first apartment. I didn't really know how to grocery shop… so I was always buying junk food/pre made food. And I also thought you had a little bit more time to pay rent; until I got served with papers for being about 2 weeks late. But you live and learn as you get older. In this day making it to your next birthday is a major blessing. I'm not sure if I'm going to have children, but I definitely want to break generational curses and pass my knowledge along to anyone that's going to listen and take heed. Life is meant to be experienced… the good, the bad, and the ugly. No one has it all figured it out and if they say they do… they're lying. As cliché as it might sound, life is about the journey and not the destination. That was so old of me to say, but it's facts. My daddy has always told me, "Keep on living." With those words, I will. When I was younger I honestly thought you had to have it all figured it out by 25. Job, house, career. But now? Sheeeittttt… I'm about to be 34 and still tryna figure it out, and get it together. What life has taught me is there's no timeline for your journey. You get there when you get there. There are many stops and detours, but at as long as we get to the destination eventually… that's all that matters. To add to that philosophy… I also understand that God's timing is everything as well. It's a fine balance of appreciating what you have & what it took you to get to this point vs constantly wanting more and not appreciating what you have or where you are in the current moment. Gratitude and wisdom? It takes you more places than you realize. Think about what all our parents and loved ones had to go through to get where they are TODAY. Some are still struggling to survive and others are thriving. To learn from your elders and take heed of their knowledge? I feel like that's all you need. Just the comfort from an elder makes a world of difference. Could just be me, but that love, compassion, and warmth lets me know everything will be alright. Why? Because they've been through way worst shit and for them to say I'm doing okay in life? That's all the motivation I need. So if I act like an old lady with a different type of a spirit? That's because I am and my ancestors are looking after me & guiding me in the direction that I need to go. Even if I'm participating in some hoodrat shenanigans… they tap me on my shoulder and say… "I fully support".